SACREDSPACE

for Advent and the Christmas Season
2009-2010

SACREDSPACE

for Advent and the Christmas Season
2009-2010

November 29, 2009 to January 3, 2010

from the website www.sacredspace.ie

Jesuit Communication Centre, Ireland

ave maria press AmP notre dame, indiana

acknowledgment

The publisher would like to thank Piaras Jackson S.J., and Alan McGuckian S.J., for their kind assistance in making this book possible. Piaras Jackson S.J., can be contacted on feedback@jesuit.ie

Unless otherwise noted, the Scripture quotations contained herein are from the *New Revised Standard Version Bible*, copyright © 1989 by the Division of Christian Education of the National Council of the Churches of Christ in the United States of America. Used by permission. All rights reserved.

Published under license from Michelle Anderson Publishing Pty Ltd., in Australia.

Founded in 1865, Ave Maria Press is a ministry of the Indiana Province of Holy Cross.

www.avemariapress.com

ISBN-10: 1-59471-193-3   ISBN-13: 978-1-59471-193-0

Cover design by Andy Wagoner.

Text design by K. H. Coney.

Printed and bound in the United States of America.

contents

how to use this booklet

We invite you to make a sacred space in your day and spend ten minutes praying here and now, wherever you are, with the help of a prayer guide and scripture chosen specially for each day of Advent and the Christmas Season. Every place is a sacred space so you may wish to have this book in your desk at work or available to be picked up and read at any time of the day, whilst traveling or on your bedside table, a park bench . . . Remember that God is everywhere, all around us, constantly reaching out to us, even in the most unlikely situations. When we know this, and with a bit of practice, we can pray anywhere.

The following pages will guide you through a session of prayer stages.

Something to think and pray about each day this
    week
The Presence of God
Freedom
Consciousness

The Word (leads you to the daily scripture and
   provides help with the text)
Conversation
Conclusion

It is most important to come back to these pages
each day of the week as they are an integral part
of each day's prayer and lead to the scripture and
inspiration points.

Although written in the first person the prayers
are for "doing" rather than for reading out. Each
stage is a kind of exercise or meditation aimed at
helping you to get in touch with God and God's
presence in your life. We hope that you will join the
many people around the world praying with us in
our sacred space.

the presence of God

Bless all who worship you, almighty God,
from the rising of the sun to its setting:
from your goodness enrich us,
by your love inspire us,
by your Spirit guide us,
by your power protect us,
in your mercy receive us,
now and always.

Something to think and pray about each day this week:

The Quiet Life

In his classic *The Imitation of Christ*, Thomas à Kempis urges the reader to "enjoy being unknown and regarded as nothing." What he means is the ability to persist through tedium, to survive without the oxygen of recognition, praise, and stroking, to do some good things every day that are seen only by God.

Most of us start life as the center of the universe, being stroked and attended to. Baby's every smile and whimper is responded to and noted. It is an addictive experience, and it is hard to get used to being just one of a family, and later one of a whole class or school, barely noticed.

There are people, like some pop stars, who never recover from the addiction of being the center of attention, never climb out of those infantile low-lands. They find it impossible to survive without notice and applause, and spend their energies seeking it. They never fit themselves for the higher ground where the oxygen of appreciation is thinner, and they have to survive, Thomas says, unknown and hardly noticed. For all but his last three years, Jesus was happy to live a hidden life. That is where most of the good in this world is accomplished, by parents, caretakers, and all who keep going through the daily offering of their unacknowledged service.

The Presence of God
Lord, help me to be fully alive to your holy presence.
Enfold me in your love.
Let my heart become one with yours.

Freedom
Many countries are at this moment suffering
the agonies of war.
I bow my head in thanksgiving for my freedom.
I pray for all prisoners and captives.

Consciousness
At this moment, Lord, I turn my thoughts to You.
I will leave aside my chores and preoccupations.

I will take rest and refreshment in your presence Lord.

The Word

The Word of God comes down to us through the scriptures.

May the Holy Spirit enlighten my mind and my heart to respond

to the gospel teachings. (Please turn to your scripture on the following pages. Inspiration points are there should you need them. When you are ready, return here to continue.)

Conversation

Sometimes I wonder what I might say

if I were to meet You in person, Lord.

I might say "Thank You, Lord" for always being there for me.

I know with certainty there were times when you carried me.

When through your strength I got through the dark times in my life.

Conclusion

Glory be to the Father, and to the Son, and to the
Holy Spirit,
As it was in the beginning, is now and ever shall be,
World without end. Amen

Sunday 29th November,
First Sunday of Advent   Jeremiah 33:14–16

The days are surely coming, says the LORD, when I will fulfill the promise I made to the house of Israel and the house of Judah. In those days and at that time I will cause a righteous Branch to spring up for David; and he shall execute justice and righteousness in the land. In those days Judah will be saved and Jerusalem will live in safety. And this is the name by which it will be called: "The LORD is our righteousness."

- Advent tells us that we have a marvelous future awaiting us.

- What are my reactions to God's promise of great things? Do I flow easily with it? Is it drowned out by other feelings, other voices? Do my current circumstances make it hard for me to trust the promise?

- Can I listen keenly to the promise, "the days are surely coming," and step out with confidence?

Monday 30th November   **Matthew 8:5–11**

When Jesus entered Capernaum, a centurion came to him, appealing to him and saying, "Lord, my servant is lying at home paralyzed, in terrible distress." And he said to him, "I will come and cure him." The centurion answered, "Lord, I am not worthy to have you come under my roof; but only speak the word, and my servant will be healed. For I also am a man under authority, with soldiers under me; and I say to one, 'Go,' and he goes, and to another, 'Come,' and he comes, and to my slave, 'Do this,' and the slave does it." When Jesus heard him, he was amazed and said to those who followed him, "Truly I tell you, in no one in Israel have I found such faith. I tell you, many will come from east and west and will eat with Abraham and Isaac and Jacob in the kingdom of heaven."

- The centurion was a man with power and status. He was begging a favor from a penniless itinerant teacher and declaring himself unworthy even to entertain Jesus in his house.

- Jesus was amazed, not merely at the trust of the man, but at the fact that his love for his servant led him to cut through all the barriers of rank and race.

- Lord, give me the grace to break with conventions that bind me, listen to my heart, and reach out to those that I can help.

Tuesday 1st December   **Luke 10:21–24**

At that same hour Jesus rejoiced in the Holy Spirit and said, "I thank you, Father, Lord of heaven and earth, because you have hidden these things from the wise and the intelligent and have revealed them to infants; yes, Father, for such was your gracious will. All things have been handed over to me by my Father; and no one knows who the Son is except the Father, or who the Father is except the Son and anyone to whom the Son chooses to reveal him." Then turning to the disciples, Jesus said to them privately, "Blessed are the eyes that see what you see! For I tell you that many prophets and kings desired to see what you see, but did not see it, and to hear what you hear, but did not hear it."

- Thirteen centuries after Jesus, the anonymous author of *The Cloud of Unknowing* urged us in the same way to approach God in love rather than intellectual effort:

Beat away at this cloud of unknowing between you and God with that sharp dart of longing love. And so I urge you, go after experience rather than knowledge. On account of pride, knowledge may often deceive you, but this gentle, loving affection will not deceive you. Knowledge tends to breed conceit, but love builds.

Wednesday 2nd December   Isaiah 25:6–9

On this mountain the LORD of hosts will make for all peoples a feast of rich food, a feast of well-aged wines, of rich food filled with marrow, of well-aged wines strained clear. And he will destroy on this mountain the shroud that is cast over all peoples, the sheet that is spread over all nations; he will swallow up death forever. Then the Lord GOD will wipe away the tears from all faces, and the disgrace of his people he will take away from all the earth, for the LORD has spoken. It will be said on that day, Lo, this is our God; we have waited for him, so that he might save us. This is the LORD for whom we have waited; let us be glad and rejoice in his salvation.

- "He will swallow up death forever." This text of Isaiah, with its luscious imagery of fine food and wines, and of the dynamic power of the Lord wiping away our tears at the end of days, is also read at funeral liturgies.

- Our waiting for the birth of Jesus and for the joy of salvation are the same waiting—for the Lord who conquers death forever. Let us rejoice and be glad.

Thursday 3rd December Matthew 7:21, 24–27

Jesus said to his disciples, "Not everyone who says to me, 'Lord, Lord,' will enter the kingdom of heaven, but only the one who does the will of my Father in heaven. Everyone then who hears these words of mine and acts on them will be like a wise man who built his house on rock. The rain fell, the floods came, and the winds blew and beat on that house, but it did not fall, because it had been founded on rock. And everyone who hears these words of mine and does not act on them will be like a foolish man who built his house on sand. The rain fell, and the floods came, and the winds blew and beat against that house, and it fell—and great was its fall!"

- It is not enough to hear the words of Jesus. They only have power when we act on them.

- What does "acting" on the words of Jesus mean in my life? Can I actually see where my action grows out of faith and prayer?

- Do Jesus' words challenge me about times of procrastination or lack of direction when I dodge the call?

- Can I be open, right now, to hearing the will of the Father, calling me, in ways small and great, into life?

Friday 4th December   Matthew 9:27–31

As Jesus went on his way, two blind men followed him, crying loudly, "Have mercy on us, Son of David!" When he entered the house, the blind men came to him; and Jesus said to them, "Do you believe that I am able to do this?" They said to him, "Yes, Lord." Then he touched their eyes and said, "According to your faith let it be done to you." And their eyes were opened. Then Jesus sternly ordered them, "See that no one knows of this." But they went away and spread the news about him throughout that district.

- The start of this encounter is in public. Crowds are around Jesus, and the blind men are caught up in the general emotion. They shout at Jesus using a formal title, "Son of David," as though he were a powerful messianic figure dispensing health to crowds.

- Jesus waits until he is in the house, where he can meet the blind men in person and question their faith.

Saturday 5th December   **Isaiah 30:19–21**

Truly, O people in Zion, inhabitants of Jerusalem, you shall weep no more. He will surely be gracious to you at the sound of your cry; when he hears it, he will answer you. Though the Lord may give you the bread of adversity and the water of affliction, yet your Teacher will not hide himself any more, but your eyes shall see your Teacher. And when you turn to the right or when you turn to the left, your ears shall hear a word behind you, saying, "This is the way; walk in it."

- "The bread of adversity and the water of affliction" could sound like food, however plain. They do not taste like that when we lose a job, fall ill, lose the affection of friends, or suffer deeply. Then it seems all destructive and wrong.

- But your eyes shall see your Teacher. Your ears shall hear a word behind you, saying, "This is the way; walk in it."

december 6–12, 2009

Something to think and pray about each day this week:

Making Preparations

Twice in the year, at Advent and Lent, we spend weeks preparing our souls for a great feast. Try imagining the preparation that Mary made. She spent three months helping her cousin Elizabeth with an unexpected pregnancy. Then she had to face the awful crisis with Joseph, who could not understand how she could be pregnant (Matthew 1:19). Then when things seemed to be on an even course for the birth, she found they had to pull up roots, harness the donkey, and trek up to Bethlehem, where they could find no room in the inn. Mary's main preparation was adjusting to what was unexpected and unwished-for.

The Presence of God

God is with me, but more,
God is within me, giving me existence.
Let me dwell for a moment on God's life-giving
presence
in my body, my mind, my heart
and in the whole of my life.

Freedom

God is not foreign to my freedom.
Instead the Spirit breathes life into my most inti-
mate desires,
gently nudging me toward all that is good.
I ask for the grace to let myself be enfolded by the
Spirit.

Consciousness

Help me, Lord, to be more conscious of your
presence.
Teach me to recognize your presence in others.
Fill my heart with gratitude for the times your love
has been shown to me through the care of others.

The Word

I read the Word of God slowly, a few times over,
and I listen to what God is saying to me. (Please
turn to your scripture on the following pages.

Inspiration points are there should you need them.
When you are ready, return here to continue.)

Conversation

How has God's Word moved me? Has it left me
cold?
Has it consoled me or moved me to act in a new
way?
I imagine Jesus standing or sitting beside me,
I turn and share my feelings with him.

Conclusion

Glory be to the Father, and to the Son, and to the
Holy Spirit,
As it was in the beginning, is now and ever shall be,
World without end. Amen

Sunday 6th December, Second Sunday of Advent

Luke 3:1–6

In the fifteenth year of the reign of Emperor Tiberius, when Pontius Pilate was governor of Judea, and Herod was ruler of Galilee, and his brother Philip ruler of the region of Ituraea and Trachonitis, and Lysanias ruler of Abilene, during the high priesthood of Annas and Caiaphas, the word of God came to John son of Zechariah in the wilderness. He went into all the region around the Jordan, proclaiming a baptism of repentance for the forgiveness of sins, as it is written in the book of the words of the prophet Isaiah, "The voice of one crying out in the wilderness: 'Prepare the way of the Lord, make his paths straight. Every valley shall be filled, and every mountain and hill shall be made low, and the crooked shall be made straight, and the rough ways made smooth; and all flesh shall see the salvation of God.'"

- Who is active here? Who takes the initiative?

- If the Word of God "came" to me, would I be able to hear? What would block my hearing?

Monday 7th December   Luke 5:17–26

One day, as Jesus was teaching, there were Pharisees and teachers of the Law sitting by, who had come from every village of Galilee and Judea and from Jerusalem; and the power of the Lord was with him to heal. And behold, men were bringing on a bed a man who was paralyzed, and they sought to bring him in and lay him before Jesus; but finding no way to bring him in, because of the crowd, they went up on the roof and let him down with his bed through the tiles into the midst before Jesus. And when he saw their faith he said: "Man, your sins are forgiven you." And the scribes and the Pharisees began to question, saying: "Who is this that speaks blasphemies? Who can forgive sins but God only?" When Jesus perceived their questionings, he answered them: "Why do you question in your hearts? Which is easier, to say: 'Your sins are forgiven you' or to say: 'Rise and walk'? But that you may know that the Son of Man has authority on earth to forgive sins"—he said to the man who was paralyzed: "I say to you, rise, take up your bed and go home." And immediately he rose before them, took up that on which he lay, and went home glorifying God. And amazement seized them all, and they glorified God and were filled with awe, saying: "We have seen strange things today."

- The patient is lowered through the roof, a helpless paralytic, dependant completely on faith-filled friends.

- Forgiveness gives us the energy and dynamism to rise, take up our bed, and walk. With it comes life, and more abundantly than before.

Tuesday 8th December, The Immaculate Conception of the Blessed Virgin Mary
Luke 1:26–38

In the sixth month the angel Gabriel was sent by God to a town in Galilee called Nazareth, to a virgin engaged to a man whose name was Joseph, of the house of David. The virgin's name was Mary. And he came to her and said, "Greetings, favored one! The Lord is with you." But she was much perplexed by his words and pondered what sort of greeting this might be. The angel said to her, "Do not be afraid, Mary, for you have found favor with God. And now, you will conceive in your womb and bear a son, and you will name him Jesus. He will be great, and will be called the Son of the Most High, and the Lord God will give to him the throne of his ancestor David. He will reign over the house of Jacob forever, and of his kingdom there will be no end." Mary said to the angel, "How can this be, since I am a virgin?" The angel said to her, "The Holy Spirit will come upon you, and the power of the Most High will overshadow you; therefore the child to be born will be holy; he will be called Son of God. And now, your relative Elizabeth in her old age has also conceived a son; and this is the sixth month for her who was said to be barren. For nothing will be impossible with God." Then Mary said, "Here am I, the servant of the Lord; let it be with me according to your word." Then the angel departed from her.

- How does Mary's experience touch me? Am I called to "bear" God in my heart?

- What issues of surrender and trust arise in my case? Can I speak of these things to the Lord?

Wednesday 9th December   Matthew 11:28–30

Jesus said, "Come to me, all you that are weary and are carrying heavy burdens, and I will give you rest. Take my yoke upon you, and learn from me; for I am gentle and humble in heart, and you will find rest for your souls. For my yoke is easy, and my burden is light."

- I am often weary, Lord, and my burden feels heavy on me. When I look at Christians, some of them indeed seem relaxed and easy in your company. Others appear uptight and driven, not restful people to be near.

- You are a gentle, humble presence. If I feel under pressure in prayer, something is wrong. It is a sign of your presence to me that my soul feels rested.

Thursday 10th December   Matthew 11:11–15

Truly I tell you, among those born of women no one has arisen greater than John the Baptist; yet the least in the kingdom of heaven is greater than he. From the days of John the Baptist until now the kingdom of heaven has suffered violence, and the violent take it by force. For all the prophets and the law prophesied until John came; and if you are willing to accept it, he is Elijah who is to come. Let anyone with ears listen!

- What was it that placed John the Baptist below "the least in the kingdom of heaven"? He had preached the justice of God and the need for repentance; but he had not lived to see Jesus crucified, and in that, to see the unbelievable extent of God's love for us.

Friday 11th December   Isaiah 48:17–19

Thus says the Lord, your Redeemer, the Holy One of Israel: I am the Lord your God, who teaches you for your own good, who leads you in the way you should go. O that you had paid attention to my commandments! Then your prosperity would have been like a river, and your success like the waves of the sea; your offspring would have been like the sand, and your descendants like its grains; their name would never be cut off or destroyed from before me.

- "I am the Lord your God, who teaches you for your own good, who leads you in the way you should go." Lord, teach me to follow your paths, wherever you lead me.

Saturday 12th December   Matthew 17:10–13

And the disciples asked him, "Why, then, do the scribes say that Elijah must come first?" He replied, "Elijah is indeed coming and will restore all things; but I tell you that Elijah has already come, and they did not recognize him, but they did to him whatever they pleased. So also the Son of Man is about to suffer at their hands." Then the disciples understood that he was speaking to them about John the Baptist.

- Like John the Baptist, Elijah was a messenger of God. Like other messengers, they were shunned, ridiculed, or even eliminated.

- Advent calls us to this same journey; we risk rejection and dark times but we are promised a dawn that takes away the darkness.

december 13–19, 2009

Something to think and pray about each day this week:

Out of Nowhere

If Jesus were to appear in our world, he would be born unnoticed, to a good, struggling family in Ecuador, Uzbekistan, or some place usually out of the news. People would be puzzled, "Where is that place?" He would not be on television, nor would he occupy a center of power or wealth. He would be pushed around, slandered, and criticized. He would speak simple truths, and some would listen to him and recognize the voice of God. The good news would spread slowly, as it did two thousand years ago. It would graft onto whatever was good in the world. The brokers of power and wealth would not notice it, nor offer their sponsorship. The happy irony of today is that after the first two thousand years, the good news is so widespread that, whether they know it or not, the whole human race is richer for Jesus' birthday.

The Presence of God

What is present to me is what has a hold on my
becoming.
I reflect on the presence of God always there in love,
amidst the many things that have a hold on me.
I pause and pray that I may let God
affect my becoming in this precise moment.

Freedom

There are very few people
who realize what God would make of them
if they abandoned themselves into his hands,
and let themselves be formed by his grace.
(St. Ignatius)
I ask for the grace to trust myself totally to God's
love.

Consciousness

In the presence of my loving Creator,
I look honestly at my feelings over the last day,
the highs, the lows, and the level ground.
Can I see where the Lord has been present?

The Word

God speaks to each one of us individually. I need
to listen to hear what he is saying to me. Read
the text a few times, then listen. (Please turn to

your scripture on the following pages. Inspiration points are there should you need them. When you are ready, return here to continue.)

Conversation

What is stirring in me as I pray?
Am I consoled, troubled, left cold?
I imagine Jesus himself standing or sitting at my side,
and share my feelings with him.

Conclusion

Glory be to the Father, and to the Son, and to the Holy Spirit,
As it was in the beginning, is now and ever shall be,
World without end. Amen

Sunday 13th December, Third Sunday of Advent

Luke 3:10–18

And the crowds asked John, "What then should we do?" In reply he said to them, "Whoever has two coats must share with anyone who has none; and whoever has food must do likewise." Even tax collectors came to be baptized, and they asked him, "Teacher, what should we do?" He said to them, "Collect no more than the amount prescribed for you." Soldiers also asked him, "And we, what should we do?" He said to them, "Do not extort money from anyone by threats or false accusation, and be satisfied with your wages." As the people were filled with expectation, and all were questioning in their hearts concerning John, whether he might be the Messiah, John answered all of them by saying, "I baptize you with water; but one who is more powerful than I is coming; I am not worthy to untie the thong of his sandals. He will baptize you with the Holy Spirit and fire. His winnowing fork is in his hand, to clear his threshing floor and to gather the wheat into his granary; but the chaff he will burn with unquenchable fire." So, with many other exhortations, he proclaimed the good news to the people.

- Part of the process of preparing for the coming of Jesus is to stand among the crowd and listen to John the Baptist.

- What do I make of him? How do his words move me?

- Do I look forward to the coming of the one who will "baptize with the Holy Spirit and fire"?

- I can bring my responses and reactions to the Lord.

Monday 14th December   Matthew 21:23–27

When Jesus entered the temple, the chief priests and the elders of the people came to him as he was teaching, and said, "By what authority are you doing these things, and who gave you this authority?" Jesus said to them, "I will also ask you one question; if you tell me the answer, then I will also tell you by what authority I do these things. Did the baptism of John come from heaven, or was it of human origin?" And they argued with one another, "If we say, 'From heaven,' he will say to us, 'Why then did you not believe him?' But if we say, 'Of human origin,' we are afraid of the crowd; for all regard John as a prophet." So they answered Jesus, "We do not know." And he said to them, "Neither will I tell you by what authority I am doing these things."

- The chief priests and the elders are motivated by a desire to protect their own position and authority, and by fear—they are afraid of the crowds. Jesus, on the other hand, speaks out fearlessly, regardless of how it might jeopardize his popularity.

Tuesday 15th December   Matthew 21:28–32

Jesus said, "What do you think? A man had two sons; he went to the first and said, 'Son, go and work in the vineyard today.' He answered, 'I will not'; but later he changed his mind and went. The father went to the second and said the same; and he answered, 'I go, sir'; but he did not go. Which of the two did the will of his father?" They said, "The first." Jesus said to them, "Truly I tell you, the tax collectors and the prostitutes are going into the kingdom of God ahead of you. For John came to you in the way of righteousness and you did not believe him, but the tax collectors and the prostitutes believed him; and even after you saw it, you did not change your minds and believe him."

- Well, which am I?

- The first son sounds like a grump, hard to live with. His first reaction tended to be No. He probably suffered as much as anyone from his own grumpiness. But when the chips were down, you could trust him to help. The second son was the smiling sweet-talker. He liked to be in favor, but when he should have been working, he found something better to do— and probably a plausible excuse afterwards.

- Lord, I would rather be a grumpy but reliable helper than a sweet-talker.

Wednesday 16th December   Luke 7:19–23

John summoned two of his disciples and sent them to the Lord to ask, "Are you the one who is to come, or are we to wait for another?" When the men had come to him, they said, "John the Baptist has sent us to you to ask, 'Are you the one who is to come, or are we to wait for another?'" Jesus had just then cured many people of diseases, plagues, and evil spirits, and had given sight to many who were blind. And he answered them, "Go and tell John what you have seen and heard: the blind receive their sight, the lame walk, the lepers are cleansed, the deaf hear, the dead are raised, the poor have good news brought to them. And blessed is anyone who takes no offence at me."

- Are you the one, Lord? I am staking my life on it. I am not waiting for anyone else. Trends and fashions come and go but I am sticking with you.

- Show me how to make this world better, by tackling suffering and sickness, and reaching out to the unfortunate. In my doubts and difficulties fill my eyes with the sight of you.

Thursday 17th December   Matthew 1:1–17

An account of the genealogy of Jesus the Messiah, the son of David, the son of Abraham. Abraham was the father of Isaac, and Isaac the father of Jacob, and Jacob the father of Judah and his brothers, and Judah the father of Perez and Zerah by Tamar, and Perez the father of Hezron, and Hezron the father of Aram, and Aram the father of Aminadab, and Aminadab the father of Nahshon, and Nahshon the father of Salmon, and Salmon the father of Boaz by Rahab, and Boaz the father of Obed by Ruth, and Obed the father of Jesse, and Jesse the father of King David. And David was the father of Solomon by the wife of Uriah, and Solomon the father of Rehoboam, and Rehoboam the father of Abijah, and Abijah the father of Asaph, and Asaph the father of Jehoshaphat, and Jehoshaphat the father of Joram, and Joram the father of Uzziah, and Uzziah the father of Jotham, and Jotham the father of Ahaz, and Ahaz the father of Hezekiah, and Hezekiah the father of Manasseh, and Manasseh the father of Amos, and Amos the father of Josiah, and Josiah the father of Jechoniah and his brothers, at the time of the deportation to Babylon. And after the deportation to Babylon: Jechoniah was the father of Salathiel, and Salathiel the father of Zerubbabel, and Zerubbabel the father of Abiud, and Abiud the father of Eliakim, and Eliakim the father of Azor, and Azor the father of Zadok, and

Zadok the father of Achim, and Achim the father of Eliud, and Eliud the father of Eleazar, and Eleazar the father of Matthan, and Matthan the father of Jacob, and Jacob the father of Joseph the husband of Mary, of whom Jesus was born, who is called the Messiah. So all the generations from Abraham to David are fourteen generations; and from David to the deportation to Babylon, fourteen generations; and from the deportation to Babylon to the Messiah, fourteen generations.

- Today's readings look unsparingly at Jesus' ancestry. Matthew points out that Jesus' forbears included children born of incest (Perez), of mixed races (Boaz), and of adultery (Solomon).

- God entered into our human history with all the episodes that proud people would be ashamed of.

Friday 18th December   Matthew 1:18–24

Now the birth of Jesus the Messiah took place in this way. When his mother Mary had been engaged to Joseph, but before they lived together, she was found to be with child from the

Holy Spirit. Her husband Joseph, being a righteous man and unwilling to expose her to public disgrace, planned to dismiss her quietly. But just when he had resolved to do this, an angel of the Lord appeared to him in a dream and said, "Joseph, son of David, do not be afraid to take Mary as your wife, for the child conceived in her is from the Holy Spirit. She will bear a son, and you are to name him Jesus, for he will save his people from their sins." All this took place to fulfill what had been spoken by the Lord through the prophet: "Look, the virgin shall conceive and bear a son, and they shall name him Emmanuel," which means, "God is with us." When Joseph awoke from sleep, he did as the angel of the Lord commanded him; he took her as his wife.

- There is a model here for making decisions and dealing with doubts. Pray about it, carry it as a question, pester God about it. This is the story of Joseph's utterly unique vocation, as foster-father of the Son of God.

Saturday 19th December   Luke 1:5–25

In the days of King Herod of Judea, there was a priest named Zechariah, who belonged to the priestly order of Abijah. His wife was a descendant of Aaron, and her name was Elizabeth. Both of them were righteous before God, living blamelessly according to all the commandments and regulations of the Lord. But they had no children, because Elizabeth was barren, and both were getting on in years. Once when he was serving as priest before God and his section was on duty, he was chosen by lot, according to the custom of the priesthood, to enter the sanctuary of the Lord and offer incense. Now at the time of the incense-offering, the whole assembly of the people was praying outside. Then there appeared to him an angel of the Lord, standing at the right side of the altar of incense. When Zechariah saw him, he was terrified; and fear overwhelmed him. But the angel said to him, "Do not be afraid, Zechariah, for your prayer has been heard. Your wife Elizabeth will bear you a son, and you will name him John. You will have joy and gladness, and many will rejoice at his birth, for he will be great in the sight of the

Lord. He must never drink wine or strong drink; even before his birth he will be filled with the Holy Spirit. He will turn many of the people of Israel to the Lord their God. With the spirit and power of Elijah he will go before him, to turn the hearts of parents to their children, and the disobedient to the wisdom of the righteous, to make ready a people prepared for the Lord." Zechariah said to the angel, "How will I know that this is so? For I am an old man, and my wife is getting on in years." The angel replied, "I am Gabriel. I stand in the presence of God, and I have been sent to speak to you and to bring you this good news. But now, because you did not believe my words, which will be fulfilled in their time, you will become mute, unable to speak, until the day these things occur." Meanwhile, the people were waiting for Zechariah, and wondered at his delay in the sanctuary. When he did come out, he could not speak to them, and they realized that he had seen a vision in the sanctuary. He kept motioning to them and remained unable to speak. When his time of service was ended, he went to his home. After those days his wife Elizabeth conceived, and for five months she remained in seclusion. She said, "This is what the Lord has done for me when he looked favorably on me and took away the disgrace I have endured among my people."

- This was a red-letter day for Zechariah: He had been chosen by lot from the hundreds of available priests to offer incense for the Jewish nation. His childlessness, the great grief of his life, would have been on his mind as he prayed. The revelation that he would be the father of a special child was such an answer to prayer as to strike him speechless.

- Lord, before I existed, my parents prayed that I would be born, would live, would have a destiny with you. I thank you for the wonder of my being.

december 20–26, 2009

Something to think and pray about each day this week:

Turmoil and Joy

The word "push" is charged with meaning and memories for all young mothers. They have all had to push their infant from the warm security of the womb, through a narrow opening, into the cold and dangerous world outside mother. However painful the push, they know that the child is too big to stay and needs to move on and out. Mary knew that experience too, though it is seldom noticed in pious books (most of them written by men who have never suffered in this way). Jesus himself remarked in a parable on the contrast between the pain of childbirth and the mother's later joy that she has brought a child into the world, able to breathe and feed and live outside her body. All that emotional turmoil of pain and anxiety and joy can be read in Mary's face as she cradles baby Jesus.

se days Mary set out and went with haste
dean town in the hill country, where she
house of Zechariah and greeted Eliza-
Elizabeth heard Mary's greeting, the
her womb. And Elizabeth was filled
pirit and exclaimed with a loud cry,
among women, and blessed is the
b. And why has this happened to
r of my Lord comes to me? For
e sound of your greeting, the
ed for joy. And blessed is she
would be a fulfillment of
y the Lord."

instincts and insight of
Zechariah is baffled
foster-father Joseph
an, Elizabeth, her-
the action of the

zabeth, the in-
ppening and

The Presence of God

God is with me, but more, God is within me.
Let me dwell for a moment on God's life-giving
presence
in my body, in my mind, in my heart,
as I sit here, right now.

Freedom

A thick and shapeless tree-trunk would never believe
that it could become a statue, admired as a miracle
of sculpture,
and would never submit itself to the chisel of the
sculptor,
who sees by her genius what she can make of it.
(St. Ignatius)
I ask for the grace to let myself be shaped by my
loving Creator.

Consciousness

Knowing that God loves me unconditionally,
I can afford to be honest about how I am.
How has the last day been, and how do I feel now?
I share my feelings openly with the Lord.

The Word

I read the Word of God slowly, a few times over,
and I listen to what God is saying to me. (Please

turn to your scripture on the following pages. Inspiration points are there should you need them. When you are ready, return here to continue.)

Conversation

Do I notice myself reacting as I pray with the Word of God?
Do I feel challenged, comforted, angry?
Imagining Jesus sitting or standing by me,
I speak out my feelings, as one trusted friend to another.

Conclusion

Glory be to the Father, and to the Son, and to the Holy Spirit,
As it was in the beginning, is now and ever shall ⊮
World without end. Amen

Sunday 20th December
Fourth Sunday of A

I n those days
to a Judea
entered th
beth.
chi

I n tho
to a Ju
entered the
beth. When
child leaped i
with the Holy
"Blessed are you
fruit of your wom
me, that the mothe
as soon as I heard th
child in my womb lea
who believed that the
what was spoken to her b

- How profound are the
mothers! While husban
and struck dumb, and
has misgivings, it is a won
self pregnant, who recognize
Lord in her young cousin.

- This is a special gift given to El
timate appreciation of what is ha
who is really present.

- Do I always appreciate what is happening and who is really present? Am I open to God's gifts?

Tuesday 22nd December   Luke 1:46–56

And Mary said, "My soul magnifies the Lord, and my spirit rejoices in God my Savior, for he has looked with favor on the lowliness of his servant. Surely, from now on all generations will call me blessed; for the Mighty One has done great things for me, and holy is his name. His mercy is for those who fear him from generation to generation. He has shown strength with his arm; he has scattered the proud in the thoughts of their hearts. He has brought down the powerful from their thrones, and lifted up the lowly; he has filled the hungry with good things, and sent the rich away empty. He has helped his servant Israel, in remembrance of his mercy, according to the promise he made to our ancestors, to Abraham and to his descendants forever." And Mary remained with Elizabeth about three months and then returned to her home.

- Imagine what Mary felt as she received this awesome news. She has questions and voiced them, but she says "Yes" to God's will for her.

- Then she gives praise to God in the hymn we know as the *Magnificat*—"My soul magnifies the Lord." Can I learn from her example?

Wednesday 23rd December   Luke 1:57–66

Now the time came for Elizabeth to give birth, and she bore a son. Her neighbors and relatives heard that the Lord had shown his great mercy to her, and they rejoiced with her. On the eighth day they came to circumcise the child, and they were going to name him Zechariah after his father. But his mother said, "No; he is to be called John." They said to her, "None of your relatives has this name." Then they began motioning to his father to find out what name he wanted to give him. He asked for a writing tablet and wrote, "His name is John." And all of them were amazed. Immediately his mouth was opened and his tongue freed, and he began to speak, praising God. Fear came over all their neighbors, and all these things were talked about throughout the entire hill country of Judea.

All who heard them pondered them and said, "What then will this child become?" For, indeed, the hand of the Lord was with him.

- It would be good to stop and spend some time watching developments in the house of Elizabeth—once childless—after she has given birth to her "miracle" child.

- How must Elizabeth be feeling? How has it all impacted on old Zechariah? What about the friends and neighbors? What do they make of it?

- And what about my world? Does God break in to my life?

Thursday 24th December   Luke 1:67–79

Then his father Zechariah was filled with the Holy Spirit and spoke this prophecy: "Blessed be the Lord God of Israel, for he has looked favorably on his people and redeemed them. He has raised up a mighty savior for us in the house of his servant David, as he spoke through the mouth of his holy prophets from of old, that we would be saved from our enemies and from the hand of all who hate us. Thus he has shown the mercy promised to our ancestors, and has remembered his holy covenant, the oath that he swore to our ancestor Abraham, to grant us that we, being rescued from the hands of our enemies, might serve him without fear, in holiness and righteousness before him all our days. And you, child, will be called the prophet of the Most High; for you will go before the Lord to prepare his ways, to give knowledge of salvation to his people by the forgiveness of their sins. By the tender mercy of our God, the dawn from on high will break upon us, to give light to those who sit in darkness and in the shadow of death, to guide our feet into the way of peace."

- The *Benedictus* is a prayer of prophecy about the coming of the Savior. This "Most High" that Zechariah mentions comes not in a cloud of glory, but as a vulnerable child, with an ordinary family, in a cold stable. That is the kind of God we have.

- This babe in a manger brings light to those in darkness and takes away all my sins, doing away with the power of evil.

- What do I say to him, who loves me beyond all love?

Friday 25th December, Feast of the Nativity of the Lord   John 1:1–5

In the beginning was the Word, and the Word was with God, and the Word was God. He was in the beginning with God. All things came into being through him, and without him not one thing came into being. What has come into being in him was life, and the life was the light of all people. The light shines in the darkness, and the darkness did not overcome it.

- This introduction to John's Gospel probably incorporated an ancient hymn about Christ. It is dense and wonderful. Each phrase can be mined for treasures. "All things were made through him, and without him was not anything made that was made. In him was life, and the life was the light of men. The light shines in the darkness, and the darkness has not overcome it."

- Lord, give me a glimpse of how you infuse all things. Gerald Manley Hopkins, who meditated on these phrases, wrote:

For Christ plays in ten thousand places, Lovely in limbs, and lovely in eyes not his To the Father through the features of men's faces.

Saturday 26th December, St. Stephen, the First Martyr   Matthew 10:17–22

Jesus said to his apostles, "Beware of them, for they will hand you over to councils and flog you in their synagogues; and you will be dragged before governors and kings because of me, as a testimony to them and the Gentiles. When they hand you over, do not worry about how you are to speak or what you are to say; for what you are to say will be given to you at that time; for it is not you who speak, but the Spirit of your Father speaking through you. Brother will betray brother to death, and a father his child, and children will rise against parents and have them put to death; and you will be hated by all because of my name. But the one who endures to the end will be saved."

- Lord, I have not been dragged before governors or kings, but there have been social occasions when I felt like a sheep among wolves, and metaphorically flogged for my faith.

- When I am under pressure, do not forget me. See that I am given what I am to say and help me to be brave enough to say it.

december 27, 2009–january 3, 2010

Something to think and pray about each day this week:

Approaching a Friend

We used a word in school to describe any nice thing—it might be a cake, a good game of football, a girl you fancied, or getting off homework. We'd say: It's a gift. It fits what we have this week, a dawning year, 2010. It is God's gift, which is different for each of us. The Lord looks on each of us as he looked on Peter, James, and the others who said: We have left all things and followed you. What about us? We have done the same, and he has a future for us. W. H. Auden put it well: I want to approach the future as a friend, without a wardrobe of excuses.

The Presence of God

As I sit here, the beating of my heart,
the ebb and flow of my breathing, the movements
of my mind
are all signs of God's ongoing creation of me.
I pause for a moment, and become aware
of this presence of God within me.

Freedom

I ask for the grace
to let go of my own concerns
and be open to what God is asking of me,
to let myself be guided and formed by my loving
Creator.

Consciousness

In the presence of my loving Creator,
I look honestly at my feelings over the last day,
the highs, the lows, and the level ground.
Can I see where the Lord has been present?

The Word

I take my time to read the Word of God, slowly,
a few times, allowing myself to dwell on anything
that strikes me. (Please turn to your scripture on
the following pages. Inspiration points are there

should you need them. When you are ready, return here to continue.)

Conversation

Remembering that I am still in God's presence,
I imagine Jesus himself standing or sitting beside me,
and say whatever is on my mind, whatever is in my heart,
speaking as one friend to another.

Conclusion

Glory be to the Father, and to the Son, and to the Holy Spirit,
As it was in the beginning, is now and ever shall be,
World without end. Amen

Sunday 27th December,
Feast of the Holy Family   Luke 2:41–52

N ow every year his parents went to Jerusalem for the festival of the Passover. And when he was twelve years old, they went up as usual for the festival. When the festival was ended and they started to return, the boy Jesus stayed behind in Jerusalem, but his parents did not know it. Assuming that he was in the group of travelers, they went a day's journey. Then they started to look for him among their relatives and friends. When they did not find him, they returned to Jerusalem to search for him. After three days they found him in the temple, sitting among the teachers, listening to them and asking them questions. And all who heard him were amazed at his understanding and his answers. When his parents saw him they were astonished; and his mother said to him, "Child, why have you treated us like this? Look, your father and I have been searching for you in great anxiety." He said to them, "Why were you searching for me? Did you not know that I must be in my Father's house?" But they did not understand what he said to them. Then he went down with them and came to Nazareth, and was obedient to them. His mother treasured all these things in her heart. And Jesus increased in wisdom and in years, and in divine and human favor.

- It would be good to spend some time watching events unfold in this scene and the tension and confusion that transpires.

- At the heart of the misunderstanding was the special relationship that the boy Jesus had with the One he called his Father. Even at the end Mary and Joseph couldn't fully grasp it all.

- How am I moved by this scene? Frustrated? Angered? Touched? Hopeful?

Monday 28th December,
Feast of the Holy Innocents   Matthew 2:13–18

Now after the wise men had left, an angel of the Lord appeared to Joseph in a dream and said, "Get up, take the child and his mother, and flee to Egypt, and remain there until I tell you; for Herod is about to search for the child, to destroy him." Then Joseph got up, took the child and his mother by night, and went to Egypt, and remained there until the death of Herod. This was to fulfill what had been spoken by the Lord through the prophet, "Out of Egypt I have called my son." When Herod saw that he had been tricked by the wise men, he was infuriated, and he sent and killed all the children in and around Bethlehem who were two years old or under, according to the time that he had learned from the wise men. Then was fulfilled what had been spoken through the prophet Jeremiah: "A voice was heard in Ramah, wailing and loud lamentation, Rachel weeping for her children; she refused to be consoled, because they are no more."

- Another sad feast, remembering Herod's bloodthirsty massacre and the heartbreak of the babies' mothers. As we recover from Christmas, other parts of the world—perhaps even in our own country—are suffering bombs, bloodshed, bereavements.

- Lord, keep my heart open to the grief and tragedies that confront me.

Tuesday 29th December　　　　**Luke 2:25–35**

Now there was a man in Jerusalem whose name was Simeon; this man was righteous and devout, looking forward to the consolation of Israel, and the Holy Spirit rested on him. It had been revealed to him by the Holy Spirit that he would not see death before he had seen the Lord's Messiah. Guided by the Spirit, Simeon came into the temple; and when the parents brought in the child Jesus, to do for him what was customary under the law, Simeon took him in his arms and praised God, saying, "Master, now you are dismissing your servant in peace, according to your word; for my eyes have seen your salvation, which you have prepared in the presence of all peoples, a light for revelation to the Gentiles and for glory to your people Israel." And the child's father and mother were amazed at what was being said about him. Then Simeon blessed them and said to his mother Mary, "This child is destined for the falling and the rising of many in Israel, and to be a sign that will be opposed so that the inner thoughts of many will be revealed—and a sword will pierce your own soul too."

- Simeon waited for the Messiah, not as a conquering warlord, but as God breaking into human history in his own way. Simeon lived a life of constant prayer and quiet watchfulness, and here we have the blessed moment of recognition as he embraces the baby.

- Lord give me that grace of quiet prayer and of recognizing you when you show yourself to me.

Wednesday 30th December   Luke 2:36–40

There was also a prophet, Anna the daughter of Phanuel, of the tribe of Asher. She was of a great age, having lived with her husband for seven years after her marriage, then as a widow to the age of eighty-four. She never left the temple but worshipped there with fasting and prayer night and day. At that moment she came, and began to praise God and to speak about the child to all who were looking for the redemption of Jerusalem. When they had finished everything required by the law of the Lord, they returned to Galilee, to their own town of Nazareth. The child grew and became strong, filled with wisdom; and the favor of God was upon him.

- In this scene, Mary and Joseph are in the Temple with their child performing the rites that a poor Jewish family would.

- Anna, the holy woman who had spent years in prayer and fasting, recognized that salvation had come in this child. What did Anna see? How does she see it? Do I see it?

Thursday 31st December   John 1:1–13

In the beginning was the Word, and the Word was with God, and the Word was God. He was in the beginning with God. All things came into being through him, and without him not one thing came into being. What has come into being in him was life, and the life was the light of all people. The light shines in the darkness, and the darkness did not overcome it. There was a man sent from God, whose name was John. He came as a witness to testify to the light, so that all might believe through him. He himself was not the light, but he came to testify to the light. The true light, which enlightens everyone, was coming into the world. He was in the world, and the world came into being through him; yet the world did not know him. He came to what was his own, and his own people did not accept him. But to all who received him, who believed in his name, he gave power to become children of God, who were born, not of blood or of the will of the flesh or of the will of man, but of God.

- In this hymn that introduces the fourth Gospel, John proclaims the faith that marks us as Christian. We believe that Jesus is the Word of God, his perfect expression. "No one has ever seen God. It is God the only Son, who is close to the Father's heart, who has made him known."

- Lord, let me grow in the knowledge of God. May I receive of your fullness, grace upon grace. You took on this mortal flesh for me and lived among us. May this coming year bring me closer to you.

Friday 1st January, Solemnity of Mary, Mother of God   Luke 2:16–21

So they went with haste and found Mary and Joseph, and the child lying in the manger. When they saw this, they made known what had been told them about this child; and all who heard it were amazed at what the shepherds told them. But Mary treasured all these words and pondered them in her heart. The shepherds returned, glorifying and praising God for all they had heard and seen, as it had been told them. After eight days had passed, it was time to circumcise the child; and he was called Jesus, the name given by the angel before he was conceived in the womb.

- We celebrate the most passionate and enduring of all human relationships, that of mother and child. As Mary looked at her baby and gave him her breast, she knew that there was a dimension here beyond her guessing.

- Christians thought about it for four centuries before they dared to consecrate the title, Mother of God. Like Mary, I treasure the words spoken about Jesus, and ponder them in my heart.

Saturday 2nd January · John 1:22–28

Then the priests and Levites said to John, "Who are you? Let us have an answer for those who sent us. What do you say about yourself?" He said, "I am the voice of one crying out in the wilderness,

'Make straight the way of the Lord,'" as the prophet Isaiah said. Now they had been sent from the Pharisees. They asked him, "Why then are you baptizing if you are neither the Messiah, nor Elijah, nor the prophet?" John answered them, "I baptize with water. Among you stands one whom you do not know, the one who is coming after me; I am not worthy to untie the thong of his sandal." This took place in Bethany across the Jordan where John was baptizing.

- John is the last of the great prophets, and he is causing a stir; the authorities are agitated by his baptizing.

- But John leaves them in no doubt about his mission. He is but a "voice" preparing the way; there is another already among them who is "the one." He, John, is not even "worthy to untie the thong of his sandal."

- The time is now.

Sunday 3rd January,
The Epiphany of the Lord   Matthew 2:1–12

In the time of King Herod, after Jesus was born in Bethlehem of Judea, wise men from the East came to Jerusalem, asking, "Where is the child who has been born king of the Jews? For we observed his star at its rising, and have come to pay him homage." When King Herod heard this, he was frightened, and all Jerusalem with him; and calling together all the chief priests and scribes of the people, he inquired of them where the Messiah was to be born. They told him, "In Bethlehem of Judea; for so it has been written by the prophet: 'And you, Bethlehem, in the land of Judah, are by no means least among the rulers of Judah; for from you shall come a ruler who is to shepherd my people Israel.'" Then Herod secretly called for the wise men and learned from them the exact time when the star had appeared. Then he sent them to Bethlehem, saying, "Go and search diligently for the child; and when you have found him, bring me word so that I may also go and pay him homage." When they had heard the king, they set out; and there, ahead of them, went the star that they had seen at its rising, until it stopped over the place where the child was. When they saw that the star had stopped, they were overwhelmed with joy. On entering the house, they saw the child with Mary his mother; and they knelt down and paid him homage. Then, opening their treasure chests, they offered him gifts of gold, frankincense, and myrrh. And having been warned in a dream not to return to Herod, they left for their own country by another road.

- I love the Bavarian custom of chalking "G M B" for Gaspar, Melchior, and Balthasar on the wall of each room of the house on Epiphany morning. These are the names that tradition assigns to the Magi, representing all the nations of the world.

- As more and more people move to our shores and come into our neighborhoods and homes, do they discover you there, Lord? If justice and love are to be found in my home, then visitors, like the Magi, will be overwhelmed with joy and pay you homage.

introduction to the advent retreat

Christianity affirms that a man, Jesus Christ, is at the same time God. In this it stands alone among the religions of the world. Christians claim that the God of the Jews, the Muslims, of all the great world religions, has become incarnate in a man, Jesus of Nazareth. This presents a difficulty to Muslim and Jewish people, and to all religions and pious people of yesterday and today who venerate and adore a transcendent God—a God who is totally other, a God beyond this world, infinite, eternal, incomprehensible, and above everything that human beings can be and know.

Advent is a good time to pray and reflect on this central truth of the Christian religion. By doing so, we can learn something about the meaning of our own lives, of our roots, and of true humanity. By meditating on the human life of Jesus Christ, God becomes human for us, we discover that our lives have a purpose and a goal, summed up in the newborn child, Jesus. If you want to see what our God is like, look into the manger.

Time

It takes time to take in such a radical truth because it takes God time to bring the truth about God home to us. To find the time to spend with God we will have to take time from something else, be it listening to the radio or to music, watching TV, texting, phoning, or partying with our friends.

Place

Time isn't all you'll require. You will also need to choose a place to spend time with God. Of course we can pray anywhere, just as we can spend time with friends anywhere. But some places are better than others when it comes to spending time with a friend. On a bus or in a car is better than on a bicycle, on a walk is better than a noisy pub! A place where you can be alone with your friend and not be interrupted is best. If you are to spend "quality time" with God, it is best to find a place where you can be alone and not be interrupted. You may have to experiment to find somewhere that works for you; when you do, stick to it.

Decisions

Three decisions are required as you approach this retreat:

1) To make this Advent Retreat you have to decide to commit to making three periods of prayer and reflection between now and Christmas Day.

2) Having decided to make the Retreat, you will have to decide whether you will devote a particular day to the Retreat, or devote some time on each of three separate days.

3) You will have to decide how long you will spend on each prayer period. It is best to fix the length of time, be it thirty, forty, fifty, or sixty minutes, and commit beforehand to not reducing the time decided. You can always increase the time, of course!

Now you are ready to go!

Advent

Advent is about waiting and wanting. All of the Advent people are waiting: Zechariah and Elizabeth are waiting, Mary and Joseph are waiting, Simeon and Anna are waiting. We are invited to wait, to want. We are invited to get in touch with our longing for someone or something to come along and bring new meaning into our lives. Jesus, God made man, was born in ordinary surroundings so there is no need to look for the extraordinary, the spectacular, or the miraculous during Advent. God can be found where we live; in our kitchens, at our tables, in our places of work, in each others' faces. There was no prior publicity regarding his coming, no expensive advertising, no claim to privilege, just a silent, humble entry. Jesus' coming into any life will be similar. Be ready to be surprised. We tend to look for Jesus everywhere, except in the place where the incarnation took place: our flesh. Incarnation means taking flesh, and by taking flesh, Christ entered into ordinary life and invited us to meet Him there.

Two Retreat Options
Option 1: A one-day retreat
Option 2: One prayer session on each of three days

Option 1: One-Day Retreat

Make yourself a timetable for the day. Here is a suggestion that you can adapt to suit your circumstances.

9:30am: *Preparation:* Take some time to prepare a place for your prayer; have the scripture passages you propose to use to hand; recall you are spending the day with God; write down what you want from the day, what you hope will happen.

10:00am: *First Prayer Session* (Luke 1:26–37)

11:00am: *Break:* take a stretch, walk around, have some refreshment, review the prayer period.

11:30am: *Second Prayer Session* (Luke 1:39–56)

12:30pm: *Lunch Break:* take time to eat and review the prayer period.

2:30pm: *Third Prayer Session* (Matthew 1:18–25)

3:30pm: *Break:* take a stretch, walk around, have some refreshment, review the prayer period.

4:00pm: *Review the day.*

Option 2: One Prayer Session over Three Days

Preparation: 15 minutes

Prayer Session: 60 minutes (or whatever you decided)

Review of prayer period: 15 minutes

first prayer session

Getting Started:
Go to the place you have decided on for your prayer. Rather than drift into prayer, indicate to yourself that you are beginning your prayer. You might, for example, make the sign of the cross or bow. Take up a posture that helps you stay in touch with God. Try to become quiet, still, exteriorly and interiorly.

Presence

Recall that you want to get in touch with a Person, and that that Person is God: Father, Son, and Holy Spirit. Recall too that God wants to get in touch with you.

Become present to each other; notice God noticing you. How does God look at you? How do you look at God?

Companion in Prayer

Ask the Holy Spirit for help in your prayer. "Come Holy Spirit, teach me to pray; help me to do it."

Desire

Get in touch with what you want from God here and now, and ask for it. Do you want to know God more? To love God more? To serve God better? Deeper trust? Stronger hope? Forgiveness? Compassion?

Read and Reread the scripture passage slowly, pausing wherever and whenever you feel drawn to do so.

luke 1:26–37

I n the sixth month the angel Gabriel was sent by God to a town in Galilee called Nazareth, to a virgin engaged to a man whose name was Joseph, of the house of David. The virgin's name was Mary. And he came to her and said, "Greetings, favoured one! The Lord is with you." But she was much perplexed by his words and pondered what sort of greeting this might be. The angel said to her, "Do not be afraid, Mary, for you have found favour with God. And now, you will conceive in your womb and bear a son, and you will name him Jesus. He will be great, and will be called the Son of the Most High, and the Lord God will give to him the throne of his ancestor David. He will reign over the house of Jacob for ever, and of his kingdom there will be no end." Mary said to the angel, "How can this be, since I am a virgin?" The angel said to her, "The Holy Spirit will come upon you, and the power of the Most High will overshadow you; therefore the child to be born will be holy; he will be called Son of God. And now, your relative Elizabeth in her old age has also conceived a son; and this is the sixth month for her who was said to be barren. For nothing will be impossible with God."

Keeping Going

- Create the event described above in your own imagination. Imagine the place—just as many an artist has done—where this occurred.

- Recall who is involved—Gabriel and Mary. Anybody else? What about you? God became human for your sake so you are involved too. Put yourself in the picture.

- Listen to what the persons are saying—to Gabriel and to Mary. Do you want to say anything to either of them? Perhaps you want just to be there noticing what is going on, marvelling at it, wondering at how God does things.

Reflections

Mary has not yet moved in to live with her husband, Joseph. She is a virgin. What is happening to her is not a response to her yearning for a child but a surprise initiative by God which neither she nor Joseph could have anticipated. Mary is the first to hear the Good News—that God so loves the world that He wants to send His only Son as Saviour, as Messiah. Mary is the first to accept the Good News, "I am the handmaid of the Lord," said Mary, "let what you have said be done to me." To have said "Yes" to God on this occasion, Mary must have said "Yes" to God before this. To say "Yes" to God on this occasion, Mary must believe Gabriel when he says that nothing is impossible to God. Mary is blessed not because she is a giver but because she is a receiver.

We prefer to think of ourselves as givers. Perhaps there's not too much wrong with that except that it's a direct contradiction of the biblical account of the first Christmas. We had little to do with God's work in Jesus. We didn't think of it, understand it, or approve it. All we can do is, like Mary, receive it—a gift from a God we hardly know! With God we are always receivers. It's tough to be on the receiving end of love, God's or anybody else's. It requires that we see our lives not as our possessions, but as gifts. That is humbling!

Lord, help me to be like Mary, a receiver of your gifts, to realise that the greatest gift I can give to you is, like Mary, say "Yes" to the gifts you have given, continue to give, and want to give me.

Review of Prayer Period

How did you get on? Was the prayer time easy or difficult? What was easy about it? What was difficult? If it was easy, give thanks. If it was difficult, remember that trying to pray is praying. The important thing is never to give up trying. If you were to repeat this period of prayer, what would you change, if anything? Keep a few notes as you may want to repeat this prayer and return to the easy and/or difficult bits.

second prayer session

Getting Started:

Go to the place you have decided on for your prayer. Rather than drift into prayer, indicate to yourself that you are beginning your prayer. You might, for example, make the sign of the cross or bow. Take up a posture that helps you be in touch with God. Try to become quiet, still, exteriorly and interiorly.

Presence

Recall that you want to get in touch with a Person,
and that that Person is God—Father, Son, and
Holy Spirit. Recall too that God wants to get in
touch with you.

Become present to each other; notice God noticing you. How does God look at you? How do you
look at God?

Companion in Prayer

Ask the Holy Spirit for help in your prayer. "Come
Holy Spirit, teach me to pray; help me to do it."

Desire

Get in touch with what you want from God here
and now, and ask for it. Do you want to know
God more? To love God more? To serve God better? Deeper trust? Stronger hope? Forgiveness?
Compassion?

Read and Reread the scripture passage slowly,
pausing wherever and whenever you feel drawn to
do so.

Scripture Passage
luke 1:39–56

In those days Mary set out and went with haste to a Judean town in the hill country, where she entered the house of Zechariah and greeted Elizabeth. When Elizabeth heard Mary's greeting, the child leapt in her womb. And Elizabeth was filled with the Holy Spirit and exclaimed with a loud cry, "Blessed are you among women, and blessed is the fruit of your womb. And why has this happened to me, that the mother of my Lord comes to me? For as soon as I heard the sound of your greeting, the child in my womb leapt for joy. And blessed is she who believed that there would be a fulfillment of what was spoken to her by the Lord." And Mary said,

"My soul magnifies the Lord,
and my spirit rejoices in God my Saviour,
for he has looked with favour on the lowliness of his servant.
Surely, from now on all generations will
call me blessed;

for the Mighty One has done great things
for me,
and holy is his name.
His mercy is for those who fear him
from generation to generation.
He has shown strength with his arm;
he has scattered the proud in the thoughts
of their hearts.
He has brought down the powerful from
their thrones,
and lifted up the lowly;
he has filled the hungry with good things,
and sent the rich away empty.
He has helped his servant Israel,
in remembrance of his mercy,
according to the promise he made to our
ancestors,
to Abraham and to his descendants
forever."

And Mary remained with her for about three months and then returned to her home.

Keeping Going

- Create the meeting described above in your own imagination. Imagine Mary's trip to visit

Elizabeth—from Nazareth in Galilee, south to Jerusalem. Imagine their meeting, the joy expressed by both pregnant women.

- Listen to what Elizabeth and Mary are saying. Put yourself in the scene.

- Do I want to say anything further to Mary or Elizabeth, ask them for anything? Do you want to ask God for anything?

Reflections

Mary and Elizabeth are two expectant mothers, awaiting their first children. Both have experienced God intervening in their lives in extraordinary ways. Yet expecting a baby, what could be more ordinary and everyday?

Elizabeth says that Mary is blessed. Why? Because she is the mother of a Son, who is also God's Son, the Messiah? Any other reason why she is blessed? She is doubly blessed because she not only heard the word of God but she believed it. You can't be God's Son's mother but you can hear the word of God, believe it, and live it. Do you want to say anything to either of them? Want to ask to believe that God is working in your life too, intervening in it? Perhaps you want just to be there noticing what is going on, marvelling at it, wondering at how God does things. Mary understands that what has happened to her is Good News, for her and for all people. Can you interpret for yourself, and others, what happens at Christmas so that you, and they, will recognise it as Good News?

Review of Prayer Period

How did you get on? Was the prayer time easy or difficult? What was easy about it?

What was difficult? If it was easy, give thanks. If it was difficult, remember that trying to pray is praying. The important thing is never to give up trying. If you were to repeat this period of prayer, what would you change, if anything? Keep a few notes as you may want to repeat this prayer and return to the easy and/or difficult bits.

third prayer session

Getting Started:

Go to the place you have decided on for your prayer. Rather than drift into prayer, indicate to yourself that you are beginning your prayer, e.g., make the sign of the cross or bow, and take up a posture that helps you be in touch with God. Try to become quiet, still, exteriorly and interiorly.

Presence

Recall that you want to get in touch with a Person, and that that Person is God—Father, Son, and Holy Spirit. Recall too that God wants to get in touch with you.

Become present to each other; notice God noticing you. How does God look at you? How do you look at God?

Companion in Prayer

Ask the Holy Spirit for help in your prayer. "Come Holy Spirit, teach me to pray; help me to do it."

Desire

Get in touch with what you want from God here and now, and ask for it. Do you want to know God more? To love God more? To serve God better? Deeper trust? Stronger hope? Forgiveness? Compassion?

Read and Reread the scripture passage slowly, pausing wherever and whenever you feel drawn to do so.

matthew 1:18–25

N ow the birth of Jesus the Messiah took place in this way. When his mother Mary had been engaged to Joseph, but before they lived together, she was found to be with child from the Holy Spirit. Her husband Joseph, being a righteous man and unwilling to expose her to public disgrace, planned to dismiss her quietly. But just when he had resolved to do this, an angel of the Lord appeared to him in a dream and said, "Joseph, son of David, do not be afraid to take Mary as your wife, for the child conceived in her is from the Holy Spirit. She will bear a son, and you are to name him Jesus, for he will save his people from their sins." All this took place to fulfill what had been spoken by the Lord through the prophet:

"Look, the virgin shall conceive and
bear a son,
and they shall name him Emmanuel,"

which means, "God is with us." When Joseph awoke from sleep, he did as the angel of the Lord commanded him; he took her as his wife, but had no marital relations with her until she had borne a son; and he named him Jesus.

Keeping Going

- Create the event described above in your own imagination. Imagine the place—as an artist might do—imagine where the event takes place. Put yourself there too.

Reflections

Imagine Joseph's dilemma prior to the dream. Since he was not the father of Mary's child, there were only two possibilities—either Mary had been unfaithful to their engagement or she had been forced against her will, and so was innocent. But should he make a public spectacle of Mary by insisting on a formal enquiry to establish the truth? He had decided not to insist on an enquiry but to divorce her quietly. In Matthew's Gospel there is no "annunciation" to Mary. The "annunciation" is to Joseph, in a dream, telling him not to divorce Mary, as he had decided, but to complete the marriage process and take her to his house, because her pregnancy was of the Holy Spirit. He was not the father of Mary's baby but nor was any man.

What the angel tells Joseph changes everything. He takes Mary to his house, completes the marriage process, and when Mary's baby is born he names him Jesus, thereby declaring that he is Jesus' legal father. What's in a name? Jesus means "saviour"; Jesus was also called "Emmanuel" which means, "God-is-with-us." "I am with you always to the end of the world" (Matthew 28:20).

What kind of a man, of a father, was Joseph? A believer of God's word? A hearer and doer of that word, like Mary? Upright? Honest with himself and with Mary? Sensitive? Loving? Thoughtful? Think of what he did subsequently for his son, the flight into Egypt, the return from Egypt when it was safe for the child, his reaction to the loss of Jesus in the Temple.

Talk to Joseph about his dilemma and how he resolved it. What of your own dilemmas? Would he be a good person with whom to talk about them? Ask his help to believe, as he did, that God knows our dilemmas, wants to help us. Ask to be able to hear God's help.

Review of Prayer Period

How did you get on? Was the prayer time easy or difficult? What was easy about it?

What was difficult? If it was easy, give thanks. If it was difficult, remember that trying to pray is praying. The important thing is never to give up trying. If you were to repeat this period of prayer, what would you change, if anything? Keep a few notes as you may want to repeat this prayer and return to the easy and/or difficult bits.

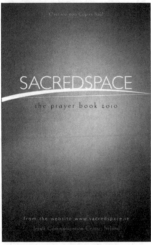